ICONIC DESIGNS

GREAT
CAR
DESIGNS

1900–TODAY

Richard Spilsbury

heinemann
raintree

© 2016 Heinemann-Raintree
an imprint of Capstone Global Library, LLC
Chicago, Illinois

To contact Capstone Global Library please call 800-747-4992, or visit our web site www.capstonepub.com

Edited by Clare Lewis and Abby Colich
Designed by Richard Parker
Original illustrations © Capstone Global Library 2015
Illustrated by HL Studios
Picture research by Jo Miller
Production by Victoria Fitzgerald
Originated by Capstone Global Library Ltd.
Printed and bound in China by Leo Paper Products

19 18 17 16 15
10 9 8 7 6 5 4 3 2 1

Library of Congress Cataloging-in-Publication Data
Spilsbury, Richard, 1963-
  Great car designs 1900-today / Richard Spilsbury.
    pages cm.—(Iconic designs)
  Includes bibliographical references and index.
  ISBN 978-1-4846-2617-7 (hb)—ISBN 978-1-4846-2622-1 (pb)—ISBN 978-1-4846-2632-0 (ebook) 1.
Automobiles—History—Juvenile literature. I. Title. II. Title: Great car designs nineteen hundred-today.
  TL147.S674 2015
  629.222—dc23   2015000281

Acknowledgments
We would like to thank the following for permission to reproduce photographs: Alamy: AF archive, 12, Bill Philpot, 22, Heritage Image Partership Ltd/National Motor Museum, 21, Ian Macpherson, 27, Motoring Picture Library, cover, 8, 16, 30, ZUMA Press, Inc, 15; Corbis: Bettmann, 6, Car Culture, 36, Transtock/Johm Lamm, 35; Getty Images: Car Culture, 26, Heritage Images/National Motor Museum, 7, The LIFE Picture Collection/Timepix/Hugo Jaeger, 10; Landov: DPA/ULI DECK, 13, Reuters/Ina Fassbender, 32; Newscom: akg-images/Paul Almasy, 18, ImageBROKER/Martin Mozter, 17, MCT/David M. Warren, 42, NI Syndication, 14, WENN/CB2/ZOB, 39, ZUMA Press/ChinaFotoPress, cover (inset), 43, ZUMA Press/Jean-Francois Galeron, 29, ZUMA Press/Sutton Motorsports, 28; Rex USA: Paul Cooper, 40; Shutterstock: Fedor Selivanov, 24, gallimaufry, 5, Maksim Toome, 23, Natursports, 4; SuperStock: LUCASFILM/20TH CENTURY FOX/Album, 33; Wikimedia, 9, dave_7, 11, Traction.fr, 20

Design Elements
Shutterstock: franco's photos, Jason Winter, URRRA

CONTENTS

Some words are shown in bold, **like this**. You can find out what they mean by looking in the glossary.

INTRODUCING ICONIC CARS

Imagine a world without cars. Difficult to picture, isn't it? Cars are one of our most convenient forms of transportation. They come in an amazing variety of shapes, colors, and styles, and all of them are the products of designers.

Car design

Any car design starts with a product **specification**. This is a detailed list of answers to questions such as these:

- What is the car's function—for example, luxury limousine or military SUV?
- What is its form or shape—for example, a sleek or boxy shape?
- What materials will it use—for example, plastic, glass, or metal?
- How much will it cost?

The design for a race car needs to be different from a taxi, because they have different functions.

CAR EVOLUTION

The first car or practical horseless carriage was built by Karl Benz in 1885. It was a carriage with three wheels and a small gasoline engine. Benz's car had a top speed of about 8 miles (13 kilometers) per hour. Since then, there have been many major changes such as an extra wheel, greater power, and air-filled tires for comfort driving over bumps.

Car designers also need to cover the basics, such as making the car safe to drive. Cars need good brakes and air bags to protect passengers. All cars take a long time to develop from the first idea or **concept**. That's because carmakers continually test designs and make improvements.

WHAT iS AN iCONiC CAR?

Iconic cars are the most famous cars. Some are famous because they did something new or did it better than other cars. Some were used by many people. Some are famous because they were beautifully designed.

A car design specification may include how many passengers the car can take and how easy it is to park on crowded city streets.

MODEL T FORD

The Model T, or Thin Lizzy, was a worldwide hit and was the first popular car.

WORLD OF DESIGN

Constraints

Constraints are limits affecting design. Ford's constraints included cost and ease of use.

In the early 20th century, there were few cars and they were unreliable. Only very rich people could afford to buy them. Designer and **entrepreneur** Henry Ford changed all that when he released his Model T Ford in 1908.

Car factories today use production lines similar to Ford's. However, some of the jobs, such as painting and welding, are often done by robots!

User-friendly

The Model T was not only cheap but also user-friendly. Ford designed rugged **suspension** springs, and the car was high off the ground so that it could carry passengers in comfort on rough roads. He designed a metal cover over the moving parts underneath to stop them from getting damaged. The Model T was also easy to service. With just a few tools, it could be turned into anything from a truck to a portable sawmill!

Meeting demand

At first, Ford could not produce enough cars to meet public demand. Ford developed the car **production line** after seeing how watches and sewing machines were made by teams of workers. Each worker stayed in one place and did one job, such as bolting on a door. Trolleys carried the car from one worker to the next. This cut the time for assembling a car from 12 hours to 90 minutes, and it allowed the price to fall from $950 to $260.

CHANGING MARKET

The Model T was so successful that 15 million were sold. Ford saw no reason to change its most successful model. But by the 1920s many drivers wanted something faster and more comfortable. Sales fell, and production ended in 1927.

DUESENBERG J

The Duesenberg J was the most expensive U.S. car of its time. It cost around eight times a doctor's annual salary. For that price, customers were guaranteed extreme luxury.

The 1920s in the United States were a time of poverty for many in rural areas, but some people were getting rich. Cities were growing and people were buying more and more **consumer goods**. Those who made money from this wanted luxury goods such as fast cars. The richest of the rich could afford the iconic Duesenberg J.

Powerful and unique

The engine of the Duesenberg J was twice as powerful as any other. It could quietly speed along at up to 116 miles (186 kilometers) per hour. Customers bought the basic **chassis** and then added the bodywork. They chose the shape, from a town car to a **convertible**. They also chose finishing materials such as rare woods and fine leathers, and, in the 1930s, fittings such as radios!

Customization

Customization means to modify or build something according to individual preference. People buying new cars today can choose color, fittings, engine power, and other **customized** features.

THE BROTHERS DUESENBERG

Fred and Augie Duesenberg moved from Germany to Iowa toward the end of the 19th century. They started their careers building racing bikes and then moved on to airplane engines and race cars. After the success of the J, they built the even more powerful SJ. Sadly, Fred died when his SJ crashed. Augie failed to keep the Duesenberg car **brand** going on his own.

Volkswagen Beetle

FAST FACTS

Dates: 1938—2003
Designer: Ferdinand Porsche
Special features: air-cooled, rear engine
Top speed: 71 miles (115 kilometers) per hour
Did you know?: In total, over 23 million Beetles were made. The only cars to sell more were the Toyota Corolla and the VW Golf!

DESIGN SPECIFICATION

- Car for family of five costing less than 1,000 German marks

- Able to cruise at around 60 miles (100 kilometers) per hour in comfort along Germany's smooth *autobahns* (highways)

- **Fuel economy** of less than 1.5 gallons (7 liters) of fuel per 62 miles (100 kilometers)

- Engine cooled by air not water, and therefore not affected by freezing temperatures

- Easy to repair

The Volkswagen Beetle was first produced in 1938, just as Germany invaded Austria.

On the other side of the Atlantic Ocean, Germany was changing. In 1933, Adolf Hitler became its new leader. He started preparing Germany for war. He created jobs for people and made big improvements to the country—for example, by building new roads. Hitler realized there would be demand for a small, cheap car for Germans to get around their growing nation.

Design influences

Hitler paid Ferdinand Porsche to design the new car. Porsche's early shapes were influenced by many other small, smooth-bodied cars around at the time, including the Czech Tatra V570. Hitler sketched a shape for Porsche to base his design on, too.

The Tatra T97 was a Czech car from 1936 designed as a car for the people. Its smooth lines, rear-wheel drive, and other features provided one of several design inspirations for the VW beetle.

Changes during design

Porsche's original design was improved. A rear window was added and the engine was shifted to the back of the car, rather than the front. This made it cheaper to give the car **rear-wheel drive**. The car was originally called the Volkswagen or People's Car Model 1. It got its nickname "Beetle" due to its short, curved shape.

Wartime production

Porsche set up a new factory in Wolfsburg, Germany, to make the Beetle. But during World War II (1939–1945), the factory was mostly used to make airplane parts and missiles. It also produced military cars based on the Beetle, including the Schwimmwagen—a jeep that turned into a boat!

The rise of VW

At the end of World War II, the Volkswagen factory lay partly in ruins after being bombed by **Allied forces**. However, many machines and parts used to make the car had survived. Allied forces remaining in Germany wanted small cars, so they organized the repair of the factory. By the late 1940s, thousands of Beetles were being produced. Volkswagen, or VW, became the name of the car company.

Going global

The Beetle became a global hit during the 1950s and 1960s. The car was popular for its attractive shape, comfort, and cheap price. VW **exported** cars worldwide and set up factories in other countries, such as Brazil, to keep up with demand.

Beetles were also used to perform stunts and compete in drag races. Some were even fitted with enormous wheels to become dune buggies that could race across sand.

End of the Beetle

By the mid-1970s, there were faster small cars that were also cheaper to run than the Beetle. Sales started to drop. The German VW factory stopped making Beetles and produced the new Golf instead. But Beetles were still made in other parts of the world, such as Mexico, until 2003.

In 1997, VW released an updated Beetle. It combined the curved shape and fun character of the old one with modern features. In 2012, a redesigned Beetle (above) had a lower profile and looked more like the original Beetle.

Variations on a theme

Volkswagen used the Beetle chassis and engine for other vehicles with other functions. The VW camper had a bus-shaped body for transporting people. The Karmann Ghia had a low, sporty body for a faster drive than the Beetle.

THE JEEP

FAST FACTS

Type of car: Military vehicle
Produced by: Bantam
First produced: 1940

Many people drive jeeps today, but they were first designed as World War II military vehicles. It was a general-purpose car for shifting troops and weapons short distances. When soldiers shortened its name to "GP" and said it quickly, it sounded like "jeep"! The jeep was designed to be tough enough to travel over rough land and strong enough to have mounted machine guns. But it was also light enough to be lifted by four men or be lifted by a plane and parachuted into battlefields.

MEDAL WINNERS

Jeeps were so popular among troops during World War II that one jeep called "Old Faithful" was even given a Purple Heart (a U.S. medal awarded to those killed or injured during service) and sent home for surviving two beach landings!

Over 600,000 jeeps were built. Soldiers loved them. The jeep did everything and went everywhere. It often carried twice what it was designed for and still kept going.

RiVAL FiRMS

In June 1940, car manufacturer Bantam won the **commission** to design and build the first jeeps for the U.S. Army. The firm worked hard and fast to meet the Army's specifications. But when two rival companies, Willys and Ford, came up with their own designs, the U.S. government decided upon a standard design based on all three jeeps. The government gave the contract to make the jeeps to Willys and Ford. Bantam was left to make trailers to be used with the jeeps.

WORLD OF
DESIGN

Commission

A commission is a request to design or make something.

Modern jeeps, like the originals, are designed to be able to climb steep slopes and even cross shallow streams.

MERCEDES 300SL

FAST FACTS

Type of car: Sports car
Produced by: Mercedes Benz
First produced: 1952 (as a race car); 1954 (as a luxury sports car)

After World War II, there was more interest in small, personal cars that could be driven for fun as well as for travel. The Mercedes 300SL was originally designed as a race car. To cut down on **drag**, or **air resistance**, the Mercedes 300SL was wide and deep at the bottom but narrower higher up. This meant the sills didn't have room for door hinges. Designer Rudy Uhlenhaut and his team put the hinges on the roof. The doors opened upward, like the flapping wings of a bird!

GYMNASTIC DRIVER!

On the first **prototypes** (early versions), the door was tiny and the only way for a driver sitting inside the car to get out of it was to remove the steering wheel first and then climb up and out!

When both doors are open, it is obvious how the Mercedes 300SL got its nickname, "Gull Wing." In 1999, this iconic ride was voted "sports car of the century"!

Going public

At first, the German Daimler-Benz company had no plans to produce the 300SL for the public, but Maximilian ("Maxi") Hoffman had other ideas. Maxi **imported** Mercedes-Benz cars into the United States. He argued long and hard to persuade the company to make a sports car for his rich buyers. The 300SL was unveiled in New York in 1954 at the United States' most important car show, and crowds were wowed by a race that showcased its speed and style.

The 300SL had a luxurious leather interior.

FAST AND COMFORTABLE

The 300SL was popular among movie stars and the rich and famous not only for its smooth, sleek look and cool, race car image, but also because it was a fast and comfortable car.

CITROËN DS

At the Paris Motor Show in 1955, a new luxury French car was unveiled. The Citroën DS had a smoothly curved design that made it look like something from the future. It caused quite a stir among visitors, and 750 sold in the first 45 minutes. There were 12,000 orders for the design in the first 24 hours!

This convertible version of the Citroën DS went on display at the 1960 Paris Motor Show.

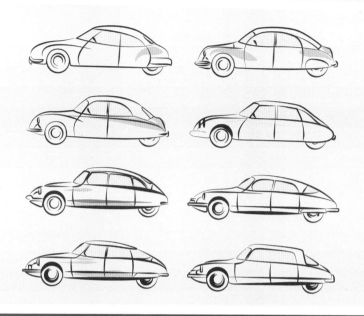

The DS design evolved from first to final ideas. But all had a smooth, **streamlined** shape with covered back wheels, to make it drive at high speeds using less power.

Automotive engineer

Person who designs, develops, and tests motor vehicles and improves parts such as engines and shape to make cars more powerful or have better fuel economy.

SKID SAVER

In 1962, French President Charles de Gaulle was traveling in a DS when some people fired guns at it. The presidential car had bulletproof glass fitted, but bullets punctured all of the tires. Luckily, the hydraulic suspension stopped the car from losing control and skidding.

Innovation

Flaminio Bertoni was the automotive engineer responsible for the modern appearance of the Citroën DS. He used human-made materials such as plastic for the roof and curved dashboard. Such materials were unusual in cars at that time. But the design hid many **innovative** technical features, too. One of these was the **hydraulic system**. This network of oil-filled tubes was used to power the steering, gear change, and for suspension. The suspension could be adjusted to make driving along France's bumpy roads a smooth experience.

Flaminio Bertoni

FAST FACTS

Dates: 1903–1964
From: Italy
Company: Citroën
Most iconic designs: Traction Avant, 2CV, DS
Did you know? Bertoni was also an **architect**.
He designed low-cost housing for St. Louis, Missouri.

Bertoni was born in northern Italy and loved drawing and sculpting. He became a car designer by accident after his father's death because he needed to leave art college and earn money to help his family. Bertoni got a job as an **apprentice** at a local carmaker. He became head designer and then set up his own design studio while continuing as an artist and sculptor.

Bertoni was a skilled sculptor. He designed the flowing shape of the Traction Avant (shown above) by shaping it in modeling clay without drawing it first.

To Citroën

Bertoni fell in love with a woman, but his family disapproved of her. The couple married and moved to Paris, France, to live. Bertoni got a job at the innovative carmaker Citroën. There, he worked closely with mechanical engineer André Lefebvrè on a new front-wheel drive car, the Traction Avant. Bertoni and Lefebvrè went on to work together on the 2CV and DS.

2CV

Bertoni's other iconic car was the 2CV. The design brief was for a cheap, small car that France's large rural population could use to get around and transport goods. Citroën requested a car with suspension capable of driving over a plowed field while carrying eggs and not breaking them. It also wanted a roof that could open up to carry large objects. The 2CV appeared in 1948 and remained in production until 1990.

Bertoni's 2CV was first designed to transport four farmers and 110 pounds (50 kilograms) of goods at 37 miles (60 kilometers) per hour to the market! But its fun design proved popular for town and city drivers, too.

1959 CADILLAC

WORLD OF DESIGN

Design influence

Design influence is the way that what is happening in the wider world can influence designs in fashion, art, transportation, and other areas.

Design is often influenced by other things going on in the world. During the late 1950s, people around the world were fascinated by the new modern jet airplanes. There was fierce competition between Russia and the United States to be the first country to get a man into space. This led to an interest in rocket-type car designs, especially in the United States. The Cadillac from 1959 was one of the most iconic.

The 1959 Cadillac Coupe de Ville weighed about 2.5 tons and was over 6 $\frac{1}{2}$ feet (2 meters) wide, but it is most famous for its extreme tail fins!

The Cadillac had several features to create a jet-like or rocket-like appearance. Its flowing design reminded people of rocket shapes. It had tall, pointed **tail fins**, inspired by the fins that stick up from the end of a fighter plane's tail to help keep a plane steady as it flies in the air. The Cadillac also had large, bullet-shaped brake lights and was covered in lots of shiny, silver chrome to give it an exciting, space-age feel.

FINISHING WITH FINS

Many cars copied the Cadillac tail fins, and tail fins grew in popularity for about a decade. People became bored with them after the United States lost the early space race in 1961, when Russia sent the first man into space.

Chrysler also designed cars with distinctive tail fins.

THE MINI

On the other side of the Atlantic Ocean, in the United Kingdom, fuel was in short supply and being **rationed**. People in the United Kingdom bought fewer new cars, but German **bubble cars** were very popular. They had high fuel economy. Then, in 1959, the British Motor Corporation introduced its own small car—the Mini. It was a huge success.

The Mini was known as the world's most advanced family car, yet it cost just $1,300. It proved to be very popular, and over one million were sold within six years. A new design of the Mini is still in production today.

Small car

The Mini was designed by Alec Issigonis. His design specification was to make a small car that was less than 10 feet (3 meters) long, of which 6 feet (1.8 meters) was space for four passengers. With its small size and light weight, the Mini could travel at 40 miles per gallon of fuel (over 6.5 liters of fuel per 100 kilometers).

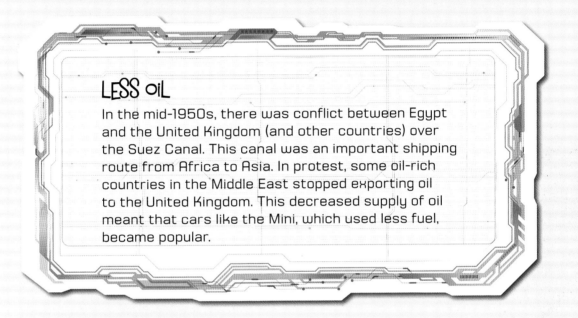

LESS OIL

In the mid-1950s, there was conflict between Egypt and the United Kingdom (and other countries) over the Suez Canal. This canal was an important shipping route from Africa to Asia. In protest, some oil-rich countries in the Middle East stopped exporting oil to the United Kingdom. This decreased supply of oil meant that cars like the Mini, which used less fuel, became popular.

Space-saving features

Issigonis used several space-saving features:

- small wheels, which needed smaller arches, taking up less interior space
- the engine mounted sideways, rather than lengthwise, under the hood
- front-wheel drive—in most cars, the engine turned the rear wheels using a bulky drive shaft
- rubber shock absorbers, rather than bulky metal springs to absorb bumps on the road
- sliding windows—the gear to roll windows up and down took up space inside the door.

E-TYPE JAGUAR

In 1961, Jaguar released a car that even today is widely thought of as one of the most beautiful cars ever built. However, the smooth shape of the E-type was not designed just to turn heads, but also to move smoothly and quickly.

This E-type Jaguar has a covered passenger compartment. Some people thought it looked a little like an airplane without wings!

Airplanes to cars

The E-type designer was an airplane engineer named Malcolm Sayer. Sayer used complex math calculations to find the best curves for the new car, just as he had done for wings and airplane bodies. His aim was to reduce drag. A smooth, pointed, streamlined shape has less drag than a rougher, flat shape. With less drag, a vehicle has better fuel economy.

Light and fast

The E-type was developed from one of the prize-winning race cars that Sayer created. It had a small, powerful engine and lightweight aluminum body to reduce weight. The E-type had a top speed of 150 miles (240 kilometers) per hour. It could accelerate from 0 to 60 miles (0 to 100 kilometers) per hour in 7 seconds.

DRAG TESTING

Sayer tested drag on early versions, or prototypes, of the E-type by taping pieces of yarn to the outside. He then drove alongside the speeding car to see how the yarn was flattened by air flowing over its surface! If there was too little flattening, he remodeled the shape to make air flow faster.

Malcolm Sayer designed many sleek, **aerodynamic** cars for Jaguar during the 1950s and 1960s, such as this C-type.

LOTUS 72

At the time when the E-type Jaguar came out, the fastest cars in the world were not on the road, but those that took part in Formula 1 (F1) Grand Prix races on tracks in 13 different countries. One of the most iconic F1 designs was the Lotus 72 from 1970.

The new nose, combined with other changes such as a large wing, made the Lotus 72 a race-winning car.

DESIGN FOR SPEED

A road car needs to be comfortable for several passengers, but race cars are all about speed for one driver. Design teams have achieved faster speeds in race cars by putting in better engines and adding rear wings to reduce drag. They have helped cars keep better control when speeding around corners by keeping weight close to the road, using airflow to pull the car toward the track, and by adding thicker tires and even extra wheels!

New shape

Before the Lotus 72, F1 cars had a hole at the front, like road cars, to take air to the engine. The air burns fuel to power the car and helps cool the engine. The trouble is that the intake causes drag. Designer Colin Chapman designed the 72 with a wedge-shaped front and no hole. The shape forced air to flow around into holes at the sides leading to the engine. This change of shape alone let the Lotus 72 go 8.7 miles (14 kilometers) per hour faster than an earlier Lotus with exactly the same engine but with a hole at the front.

GRAND PRIX WINNER

The Lotus 72 almost immediately started to win Grand Prix races. In 1970, Jochen Rindt won four in a row, but sadly, he had a fatal crash when practicing for a race. No other driver matched his points, so Rindt was declared world champion after his death. Rindt was replaced by the Brazilian driver Emerson Fittipaldi, who won the U.S. Grand Prix in 1970 and went on to be world champion in 1972 and 1973 driving the Lotus 72. In total, the car won 20 out of 75 races before its retirement in 1975, taking fifth place in the U.S. Grand Prix. By then, the 72 could not compete with the better F1 cars made by Ferrari and Brabham.

AUDI QUATTRO

The Audi Quattro is a chunky, heavy-looking car that lacks the obvious design appeal of, say, the Citroen DS or E-type Jaguar. But this 1980 car achieves its iconic status because of its fantastic road-gripping performance.

The Quattro looked very "boxy" and chunky, but drivers loved the way it handled.

Snowmobile

In the late 1970s, Audi engineers witnessed tests of a four-wheel drive off-roader developed by Volkswagen for the military and forest workers. It barely slipped on snowy roads. This spurred the Audi team to develop a four-wheel drive road car. It coped well on steep, snowy hills, but the wife of an Audi director who borrowed the prototype one weekend complained. She said the car "hopped" when cornering and was difficult to park. Designers adjusted the four-wheel drive system so that it worked perfectly. The system was driven by a **turbocharged** engine that adjusted itself via computer to work powerfully at all times.

Hand built

Quattros were expensive because of the high-specification parts inside, but also because they were handmade. Each car took seven days to build and was tested more thoroughly before sale than any other car. For example, a Quattro was tested for how waterproof it was by having water sprayed on it for 10 minutes. Most cars were tested for just 30 seconds.

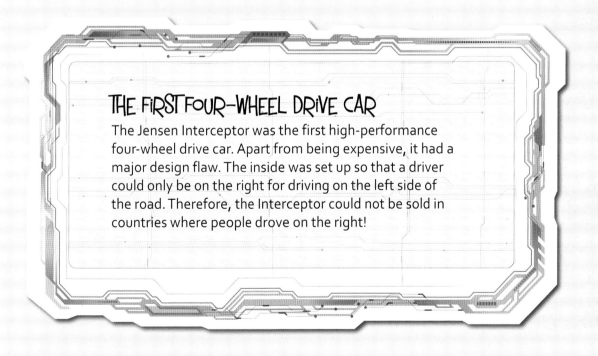

THE FIRST FOUR-WHEEL DRIVE CAR

The Jensen Interceptor was the first high-performance four-wheel drive car. Apart from being expensive, it had a major design flaw. The inside was set up so that a driver could only be on the right for driving on the left side of the road. Therefore, the Interceptor could not be sold in countries where people drove on the right!

Martin Smith

FAST FACTS

Dates: Born 1949
From: United Kingdom
Companies: Porsche, Audi, Opel/Vauxhall, Ford
Most iconic designs: 911 Turbo, Quattro, Zafira, Astra, Mondeo, Fiesta
Did you know? Smith designed Luke Skywalker's Landspeeder for the movie *Star Wars!*

Martin Smith designed the Audi Quattro in his early thirties. He wanted to be a car designer from a young age, but he was advised by Alec Issigonis to study engineering first. After receiving an engineering degree in the United Kingdom, Smith studied vehicle design and got his first job with Porsche in Germany.

A working life

Then he moved on to Audi for 20 years, followed by 7 years at Opel/Vauxhall and 10 as executive design director at Ford. In these periods, he designed the Audi 80, 100, and Quattro and the multi-person Vauxhall Zafira. He also redesigned and increased sales of many long-standing brands, such as the Astra, Mondeo, and Fiesta.

Martin Smith's engineering background has helped him create practical designs for cars.

Energy in motion

At Ford, Smith created a new "kinetic design" style. In this he used bold lines, shapes, and finishes to represent energy in motion. For example, his redesigned Fiesta had stretched headlights, a tapering, molded line down its side, and a large front grille tapering backward at its corners. These design elements made it look as though the Fiesta was moving, even when it was standing still.

Luke Skywalker's Landspeeder was one of Martin Smith's many and varied vehicle designs. It appeared in *Stars Wars* movies starting in 1977. The body shape was fitted over a smaller car to look as if the Landspeeder was floating.

TOYOTA PRIUS

FAST FACTS

Type of car: Hybrid family car
Produced by: Toyota
First produced: 1997

As people became more concerned about rising fuel prices and the **pollution** caused by burning gasoline to power cars, there was a need for a new kind of car. Toyota released its four-passenger Prius hybrid in 1997. It was the first car with a fuel-saving, less-polluting **hybrid engine** to sell in large numbers. "Hybrid" means combining two different things. A hybrid car combines a gasoline engine with an electric motor. The Prius has a distinctive wedge shape, which helps to improve the car's aerodynamics and reduce drag.

How hybrids work

- Hybrid cars use batteries to supply power to a small electric motor that drives the car in cities and on slower roads.
- They use gasoline engines to drive the car at high speeds on highways, when gasoline engines use fuel more efficiently, and to power the car if the battery runs out.
- The gasoline engine is also used to recharge the motor's battery.
- When the car is going downhill or braking, the wheels turn because of the car's **momentum** to power the electric motor and recharge the batteries.
- When more power is needed, the gasoline engine and the electric motor can even work together!

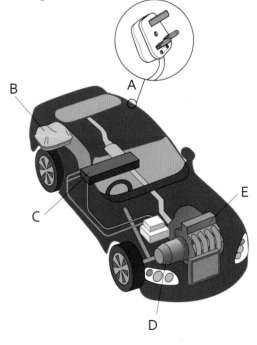

A Battery recharge plug
B Fuel tank
C Electric battery pack
D Electric motor
E Engine

WEDGE DESIGN

Part of the appeal of the Prius was its distinctive, triangular wedge shape, but designers Katsuhiko Inatomi and Norio Oseki created the wedge shape for more than looks alone. More importantly, this shape helps to improve the car's aerodynamics and reduce drag. This improves the car's fuel economy.

Another benefit of hybrid cars is that when they are running on their electric motor, they are very quiet.

Smart Car

The Smart Car is an iconic micro car that first appeared in 1998. But work on designing this vehicle began in 1972. Then there was a global oil crisis when car fuel was in short supply.

Planning for the future

The Mercedes Benz car company realized there would be demand around the year 2000 and beyond for a tiny car that used little fuel. The company designed the car to be easy to park and used in busy city streets. It also caused very little pollution, as it only needed slow top speeds.

The Mercedes Benz CCC Eco Sprinter of 1993 helped to inspire the Smart Car.

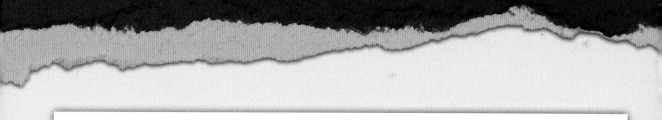

Smart Fortwo coupe
106.1 inches (269.5 cm) long

Mini Cooper coupe
145.6 inches (370 cm) long

Toyota Camry sedan
189.2 inches (480.5 cm) long

Smart Fortwo coupe
61.4 inches (156 cm) wide

Hummer H2 SUV 203.5 inches (517 cm) long

3 Smart Car parking spaces = 1 Hummer parking space

Development

Designer Johann Tomforde created several prototypes for a micro car. These included the electric NAFA car, which was never produced due to safety concerns, and the Mercedes City Car, which was taller, safer, and more powerful. By 1993, Tomforde had the basic designs for the Mercedes City Car ready. But the car did not go into production until Nicolas Hayek became involved.

DESIGN SPECIFICATION

- Short length—7 feet (2.5 meters) maximum length, making it easy to maneuver and to park. It can even be parked at right angles to the curb when space is tight!

- Space for two people and luggage

- Safe to drive—many small cars at the time were not very strong

- Economical electric or hybrid engine

Watches to cars

Like Henry Ford, Hayek wanted to make cars in the same way as watches! Hayek had invented Swatch watches and developed them into a global brand. They were cheap to make because they needed fewer parts than traditional watches. They could be easily customized with lots of colorful parts. Mercedes collaborated with Swatch, and the Smart Car brand was born.

Smart release

The first Smart Cars had tiny gasoline and diesel engines, which had the lowest **emissions** of any car engines. The first electric engines appeared around 10 years later, once they had greater reliability and battery storage. Models varied from the basic ForTwo to convertibles. Later Smart Cars included the larger ForFour (for four passengers) and faster Roadster.

WORLD OF DESIGN

Materials technologist

Person who works with materials such as metals, plastics, rubber, and ceramics. They use their expert knowledge to help engineers use the best materials for their designs.

Safe and attractive materials

All Smart Cars are built around a tough steel cage called a Tridion cell that protects passengers in the event of crashes. Recyclable plastic panels are attached on top. This material has advantages over metal because it is light, does not rust, and is bump and scratch-resistant. Also, it allows for easy customization of the color and style of a customer's Smart Car.

Smart Cars have an impressive safety history, making them both a pleasant and safe drive.

SMARTVILLE

Most Smart Cars are made in a special factory in eastern France called Smartville. It has a production line designed to reduce its environmental impact. For example, it uses powder paint rather than paint mixed with harmful chemicals to paint the car parts. It recycles heat lost from machines for warming the factory and water. It also employs nearby small companies to make the parts, which avoids the need to transport parts over long distances.

BUGATTI VEYRON

The Bugatti Veyron was named after Pierre Veyron, Bugatti's winner of the Le Mans race in 1939.

A need for speed

The Bugatti Veyron is one of the fastest cars on Earth that is allowed to drive on everyday streets (and not just race tracks). It can reach speeds of more than 250 miles (400 kilometers) per hour and accelerate to 60 miles (100 kilometers) per hour in under 2.5 seconds. Its engine is so large that it is fixed halfway along the car for balance! The Veyron's high-speed capability combined with its classic styling—large radiator, two-tone coloring, and luxurious leather interior—make this car an icon of the modern age.

Bugatti reborn

The Bugatti car company was no longer working in 1998, when the Volkswagen Group purchased the rights to use and revive the Bugatti brand. VW wanted to build a luxury car that was faster than any other, and the Bugatti name was a perfect fit, as it was already world-famous for luxury and race cars. VW presented the first Bugatti Veyron at the Tokyo Motor Show in 1999. From 2001, it made about 80 a year, for super-rich customers who usually went to pick up the cars from the factory in Alsace, France, themselves!

BRAKE POWER

In order to be safe, a fast car like the Veyron needs to be able to stop quickly. The Veyron has ceramic brakes similar to F1 cars and a **spoiler** at the back that can rise up to increase drag and help to slow the car down. The Veyron can stop from traveling at 62 miles (100 kilometers) per hour in under 3 seconds and from its top speed in 10 seconds—although the distance covered in this time is a third of a mile (half a kilometer)!

THE FUTURE OF CAR DESIGN

We have seen many iconic cars from the past and present, but what about the future? What factors and limitations will shape car designs in the future, and what might they look like?

NEW MARKETS

New cars are also being designed for rapidly **developing countries** where many people are only now able to afford them, such as India and China. The Nano Tato is a very cheap, very small car designed for city driving in India. By contrast, the Buick Lacrosse is designed for the very wealthy in China who have chauffeurs, so the focus is on roomy, luxurious backseats!

Better for the environment

The main emphasis for car designers now is on creating cars that cause less damage to the environment. The Tesla Model S is a completely electric car that can accelerate from 0 to 60 miles (0 to 100 kilometers) per hour in 5.4 seconds and creates zero emissions on the road. You can plug it in at home overnight, but until there are more recharging stations, longer journeys take some planning.

The Tesla S looks sleek and modern, makes no noise, and can be seen filling up its batteries at a charging station near you!

The Buick Envision that premiered in Beijing in 2014 is a luxury SUV. Its front grille, shiny chrome, and dynamic styling were designed for the growing group of young, rich Chinese people.

Air car

A car that runs on air sounds like it belongs in a science fiction movie, but people might be driving them sooner than you think. In 2014, Peugeot designed a new type of hybrid car, the Tata Nano, that combines a motor that runs on compressed (crushed) air with a gasoline engine.

FORMULA E

There is a new kind of motor racing called Formula E. It is for electric race cars only. The races happen in city centers and have a festival atmosphere with music and celebrities. The races could help make electric cars popular in the future.

TIMELINE

1769 The first steam-powered road vehicle is invented to move heavy cannons, very slowly

1885 Karl Benz invents the first practical horseless carriage or car with three wheels and a gasoline engine

1908 Henry Ford designs the cheap, dependable Model T Ford

1928 The luxurious Duesenberg J is released. It can be customized to the tastes of the super-rich.

1938 The Beetle, commissioned by Adolf Hitler in Germany, goes into production briefly in 1938 and then from 1945 to 2003.

1940 The Willys jeep is created for the U.S. Army for wartime use. It is a tough, small, light, all-purpose four-wheel drive vehicle used widely ever since.

1948 French car company Citroën releases the 2CV. This fun but practical car is designed primarily for the large farming population, to drive goods from fields to the market.

1954 The Mercedes 300SL small sports car is unveiled with its unusual "Gull-Wing" doors

1955 The futuristic Citroën DS is presented for the first time at the Paris Motor Show. Its design is later hailed as one of the most beautiful ever.

1959 The Cadillac, like many U.S. cars of this time, has large "space rocket" fins on its rear end

1959 Alec Issigonis designs the Mini. Its small but spacious design is popular at a time when people are worried about oil supplies.

1961 The E-type Jaguar goes on sale. This beautiful, streamlined sports car is designed by ex-aeronautical engineer Malcolm Sayer.

1970 The first wedge-fronted F1 car—the Lotus 72—starts to race. It wins 20 Grand Prix races and many other championships.

1980 The handmade Audi Quattro four-wheel drive sedan goes on sale. Its chunky design represents its hidden power.

1997 The Toyota Prius is the world's first popular hybrid engine car

1998 Smart Cars go on sale. These safe micro city cars are highly economical and easy to maneuver through congested city streets.

1999 The luxury supercar Bugatti Veyron is the fastest street-legal car on Earth

2007 Honda creates the first hydrogen car ready for production

2012 The Tesla S all-electric sports car is released to wide acclaim. It can accelerate as fast as a normal car, but is as environmentally friendly as a Smart Car.

GLOSSARY

aerodynamic describes how well something moves through the air

air resistance force of air that slows down a car or plane

Allied forces countries that fought together against Germany in World War I and World War II

apprentice person who is learning a skill while working for an employer

architect person who designs buildings

brand type of product made by a company under a particular name

bubble car small car with a clear, curved roof and often three wheels

chassis frame around which a vehicle such as a car is built

commission ask someone to create or produce something, such as a new car design

concept idea, invention, or plan

constraint restriction or limitation

consumer good something people buy, such as a TV or washing machine

convertible car with a roof that can be taken off or folded down

customize make or change something to please the owner or buyer

design influence thing that persuades a designer to design items in a certain way

developing country country that is growing richer

drag another word for *air resistance* (see above)

emission gas released into the air

entrepreneur person who makes money by starting and running new businesses

export send and sell goods to another country

fuel economy describes how far a car can travel on a certain amount of fuel

hybrid engine engine that combines a gasoline engine with another type of engine, such as an electric motor

hydraulic system machine that works by using the force created by pushing a liquid through pipes

import bring in and buy goods from another country

innovative describes a new, original idea or way of doing something

momentum tendency of an object to keep moving in the same direction

pollution when air, water, and other parts of the environment are contaminated or made dirty by waste, chemicals, and other harmful substances

production line line of workers and machines in a factory working on different stages of the same product

prototype first version of a design, which is usually improved upon in later designs

ration limit the amount of something someone can have

rear-wheel drive system that provides power to the rear (back) wheels of a vehicle

specification detailed description of how a design or something else should be done

spoiler part that is raised up on the back of a car or plane to increase its air resistance

streamlined shaped to reduce air resistance and move through the air easily and quickly

suspension system of springs and shock absorbers supporting a vehicle on its wheels, which makes it more comfortable to drive and ride in

tail fin part that sticks up at the end of a vehicle. The fin helps to keep it steady when it moves or is there for decoration.

turbocharged when a vehicle is fitted with a device that makes it faster and more powerful

FIND OUT MORE

Books

Arnold, Nick. *How Cars Work*. Philadelphia: RP Kids, 2012.

Economy, Peter. *New Car Design*. Novato, CA.: Treasure Bay, 2010.

Graham, Ian. *Cars* (Design and Engineering). Chicago: Heinemann Library, 2013.

Hammond, Richard. *Car Science.* New York: Dorling Kindersley, 2008.

Internet Sites

Facthound offers a safe, fun way to find Internet sites related to this book. All of the sites on Facthound have been researched by our staff.

Here's all you do:

Visit www.facthound.com

Type in this code: 9781484626177

Places to visit

The Henry Ford
20900 Oakwood
Dearborn, Michigan 48124
Tel: (313) 982-6001
E-mail: use the form at www.thehenryford.org/about/contact.aspx
Web site: www.thehenryford.org

At this museum, you can see over 140 vehicles on display and learn more about the amazing changes that Henry Ford's innovations brought to the United States and the world.

National Auto Museum
10 South Lake Street
Reno, Nevada 89501
Tel: (775) 333-9300
E-mail: use the form at www.automuseum.org/contact-us
Web site: www.automuseum.org
This museum has an amazing collection of over 200 cars, telling the history of car design from early cars to the present.

Petersen Automotive Museum
6060 Wilshire Boulevard
Los Angeles, California 90036
Tel: (323) 930-2277
E-mail: info@petersen.org
Web site: www.petersen.org
This museum focuses on the role of cars in American life and culture.

Ideas for research

If you would like to be a car designer one day, then visit:
www.theartcareerproject.com/automobile-design-career/584/ to learn more about this career path.
Find out as much as you can about product design; there are some fascinating interviews with designers at:
www.cardesignnews.com/site/designers/designer_interviews/.

INDEX